Brent James was educated in Sydney, Australia in an opportunity class for talented children and loved it. He then moved back to the UK to attend grammar school and university, studying biochemistry.

Brent has a technical bias, enjoying all things relevant to understanding the way the world works, and he also has a love of poetry, art and the written word.

Brent's favourite phrase, which he has coined himself, is:

"There is no power on Earth greater than that which can grind mountains into dust."

Brent is a fun-loving, forthright believer in the philosophy that you should always treat others as you wish to be treated yourself and he is also passionate about using his creative talents to the best of his ability.

I dedicate this work to the numerous friends, teachers and mentors that I have had the privilege to meet and work with throughout my life.

And in particular to my princess, Melanie Brewer, wherever you are… Without their love and affection at a crucial time in my life, I would not be the man I am today.

God bless you all, especially Melanie!

Brent James

LIFE'S LIKE THAT

AUSTIN MACAULEY PUBLISHERS®
LONDON * CAMBRIDGE * NEW YORK * SHARJAH

Copyright © Brent James 2024

The right of Brent James to be identified as author of this work has been asserted by the author in accordance with sections 77 and 78 of the Copyright, Designs and Patents Act 1988.

All rights reserved. No part of this publication may be reproduced, stored in a retrieval system, or transmitted in any form or by any means, electronic, mechanical, photocopying, recording, or otherwise, without the prior permission of the publishers.

Any person who commits any unauthorised act in relation to this publication may be liable to criminal prosecution and civil claims for damages.

A CIP catalogue record for this title is available from the British Library.

ISBN 9781035868957 (Paperback)
ISBN 9781035868964 (ePub e-book)

www.austinmacauley.com

First Published 2024
Austin Macauley Publishers Ltd®
1 Canada Square
Canary Wharf
London
E14 5AA

I would like to acknowledge the numerous professionals in the health service who have contributed in no small way to the healthy frame of mind that I am fortunate enough to have nurtured with their help after suffering debilitating bouts of depression following the death of my parents.

I would also like to acknowledge the love of my parents, without whom life would not have been possible.

I would also like to acknowledge Dr Ed Parkin and his surgical team from Royal Preston Hospital for saving my life against all odds.

I thank you all with all my heart.

Table of Contents

Love Must Die for a Reason	11
The Barnacle	14
Branded by the Light	16
Lost and Found	17
Jason	20
My Father	21
My Mother	22
Tragedy	23
The Waiting Room	24
Bridgette the Bicycle	25
Abandoned	26
The Tree of Life!	28
The Marie Celeste	30
One Too Many	32
Hypnos	34
Judgement Day	36
The Submariner	38
Life's Like That	40
One Day You'll Fly Away	41
The Mind of God	42
The Rain	44
The Final Curtain	47
A Leprechaun's Tale	49
New York	50
Love Is	52
Life on Mars	53
The Clockmaker	55
Devil or No	57

The Fisherman	60
My Nurse	61
A Final Prayer	62
Lost to Me	64
Tears of Salt	66
The Archangel	68
Dreams	70
Iron in the Soul	71
The Jolly Roger	73
A Time to Live	74
The Cheat	75
Feeling Blue	77
Lost Cause	78
Only the Lonely	79
The Chameleon	81
The Fist of the Rose	82
The Old Boot	83

Love Must Die for a Reason

Love must die for a reason like a flower grown extinct
It lives and dies more often than you can count or think
In oblivion we march on with the soldiers of its cause
Until we are lost forever like a solitary rose

A cenotaph is for the dead and a monument to love
Shining as brightly as the stars from up above
Offering a glimpse of what a lonely spirit Needs
To remind us all of the things on which salvation feeds
But I often see the cenotaph decked in roses red and dark
Carrying the burden on its shoulders just like the Joan of Arc
Marching off to battle for the armies of the just
All battered bruised and bloodied by loves now turned to dust
Those who die in ignorant bliss with no reverence for the past
Are missing the point of why love doesn't last
New futures replace old dreams as fast as horses in a race
And no one can predict the outcome at that relentless pace
So be careful who you choose to confide in for the ride
If it turns out to be Satan himself better run and hide
Love itself can never completely overcome
The smell of burning flesh when his unholy work is done
People would love for life if only they could see

Reflections of each other in the mirrors of
eternity
Agreeing not to differ when differences are
near
And holding hands forever when things
become unclear
I know a man who loved a woman with yearning
deep inside
She was a tower of strength reason poetry
and pride
They were both wrapped in glass though
little did they know
An earthquake would give rise to the debris
down below
Their inscription reads like Babel's dream
of living in the place
Of infinite glory fulfilment and God's
forgiving grace
On and on it went as they drank love's
potion deep
Strong enough to bring about collapse and
put them both to sleep
Be it longevity is your forte I beg to ask you
why
You don't stay routed to the floor instead of
reaching for the sky
Your cenotaph if you're not careful will be
a pile of bones and spit
A testament to an empty home with
darkened rooms unlit
The light consuming all will vanish if you
do not pray
And darkness will prevail until your dying
day
Only if you're sentient about your Gods
forgiving grace
Will you ever look down upon your own
beleaguered face
The cenotaph will soldier on with little or
no help from you
Reminding us of love even though our
thoughts are turning blue
Or the blackest black on days that are
warranted by need

For the poor lost souls in distant graves
where worms now breed and feed
A silent prayer will shine a light into corners
dark and deep
A beacon of hope for those who were asleep
Bringing to those who pray a feeling of
relief from grief
Like a dead olive branch that has grown a
brand-new leaf
Love must die for a reason like a flower
grown extinct
It lives and dies more often than you can
count or think
In oblivion we march on with the soldiers of
its cause
Until we are lost forever like a solitary rose!

The Barnacle

I once knew a man with a will wrought from brass
Who consistently struggled because he was working class
He climbed out of bed every morning at six
To work hard and pay for some mortar and bricks
The days were very long and he was good at what he did
So it wasn't long before he'd made a few quid
The house that he bought was a blessing to behold
Somewhere to live and hopefully grow old
Life is a minefield especially when you are young
So he had to be mindful not to get stung
But along came the chancellor and he couldn't believe his ears
Interest rates soared and it brought him to tears
Everyone was encouraged to buy their own place
But along came the recession and the smile fell from his face
Not an uncommon thing to get flustered and feel down
So he doubled his efforts and tried not to frown
The barnacle stuck to his rock like cement
And gave it his all to cover what was spent
But the rush of the financial tide was too Fast
He knew that his early dreams would not last
He didn't have that much left to give
And it took away one of his reasons to live
The fight for survival is an ever spinning wheel
Revolving at pace no matter how you may feel
Better if the barnacle could have weathered the tide

Instead of losing possessions and pride.
The barnacle was at sea for years or more
Until he was washed up on an unfamiliar shore
He was picked up alive by a friendly soul who said
You look like you are worth saving so it's straight off to bed
In the morning we'll see if we can help you to find
A new rock to cling to that will broaden your mind
The barnacle is me and I am a man in distress
But I am determined to think about my loss less
Barnacles are feisty tenacious and true
So I'll redouble my efforts and hang on like glue
Though my confidence and self-esteem has taken a hit
The barnacle is the man…cannot be split
The next time I cement myself to a worthy goal
I'll never let go I'll stand proud and stand tall
As for the will that was wrought from brass
It's still there and is functioning first class
I'll never give up and I'll never stop giving
To prove to myself that a life is worth living!

Branded by the Light

Lord have mercy for a peaceful man today
And listen to my words as I am about to pray
The words are meant to be a gift from me to you
A reflection of the things I see and sometimes do
I asked for the spirit to blanket me within
And keep me safe from committing unforgiving sin
When I was eight years old and still a child
Remembering that I was meek and mild
The world revolves at pace it seems
Creating and destroying dreams
The ones that last are lessons learned
Lest we forget and get our fingers burned
When I cry out in reverent pain
And search to ask why you were slain
Am I crying deep within
To relieve myself of mortal sin
The Earth wept blood the day you died
To give salvation meaning and pride
Staining you with grief and loss
Like a wounded offering upon the cross
The light of light that you inspire
Is with me now when I retire
As each day ends and I feel the heat
From bonfires lit beneath my feet
Branded by the light it seems
I pray to you and fill my dreams
With thoughts of you crying out in vain
For the world to recognise your pain
Lost in thought and in the depths of the night
I bathe in the comfort of knowing wrong from right
Struggling to stay afloat in a world awash with sin
Like an endangered species realising the trouble its' in!

Lost and Found

(After My Mother's Death)

Possessed by the Devil and consumed by his greed
I went into depression and he fed on the need
For me to self-denigrate think badly and generally ignore
That I was a victim of circumstance and nothing more
The depression was a fathomless pit full of grief
A Dante's Inferno with no shade or relief
I burned there in Hell for three years or more
Until I found myself close to death's door
Suicidal thoughts welled up from turmoil's within
To take my own life and commit ultimate sin
Thankfully the blade that I used missed my heart
And a surgeon arrived to play a vital part
That all seems like a long time ago now
And I have made a full recovery somehow
A recovery so poignant that the roses now bloom
Replacing the dark thoughts full of gloom and doom
I can't thank the church or religion as such
Because that matters to a great number of people so much
My faith has certainly played a large part
In vanquishing the demons from my wounded heart
I would rather say I believe in human nature as a force
That can shape and remould us and help to enforce
A new set of rules that everyone should follow
If we want to live for today and look forward to tomorrow
You don't plant a seed and expect it to thrive
Unless you nurture it and feed it to keep it alive
The same goes for people's ability to grow well
It's what you believe that helps you break from the spell
If you go against your nature and don't go with the grain
There is nothing but torture self-pity and pain
So I'm searching for truths about myself to unwind
The knots in my psyche and mental conflicts that I find
It's not difficult to say that I have found some relief
And it's true to say that I feel much less grief
When acceptance of loss has played a significant part
In healing what was a very broken heart
My recovery is now in the driving seat
Steering me out of the depths of defeat
To a place where I can say I belong

Making me feel content happy and strong
Abstinence from alcohol has also made me content
To look back in anger at myself and relent
From the self-punishment that dependence can bring
To a body and a mind just hell bent on one thing
To escape from the reality of what happened in the past
When things were torn down that were meant to last
Hopes and ambitions that all went astray
And have lived on it seems until this very day
It felt like the whole world had changed course
When my river of life was cut off at the source
In the same way that a river flows out to the sea
The stains on my conscience got the better of me
The inevitable happened and I had started to sink
Drowning my sorrows with the abominable drink
It took me years to shake off that affliction for good
But I am happy to say now that I feel like I should
I smile and make a song and dance these days
Because the worst of it is over and I deserve some praise
To have conquered my demons is the accolade I need
One of the challenges in life on which I now feed
I congratulate myself every day that I live
For learning the lesson of how to give
In to myself and accept that I was wrong
To think that I could live without change for so long
The spark in my life which had all but gone out
Is now back with a vengeance and I try not to shout
The wisdom of Solomon is nothing compared
To the judgement I have made for my life to be spared
An ignominious death will not do for me
I have chosen to live and forever be free
From the shackles of a burden which I carried for years
Now no more guilt uncertainty or tears
The hard part is over and the easy part can start
I'm going to enjoy this with all my heart
In the bible we live to be three scores and ten
That's what is given to mortal men
But I also know immortality can be earned with a prayer
That's if you're willing to lay your soul bare
Be honest and forthright and never give in
To the currency of corruption and the wages of sin
If I do that I will be happy in my old age
A beacon for hope in my life at this stage
Unaffected by the tragedy that I have known in the past
A house now built on rock and destined to last

My moral code my fibre my determination my will
Will all play their part and help to fulfil
A bucket list as long as Dick Whittington's dream
About creating a life made of peaches and cream
I will live in Nirvana and have time on my side
To relax and avoid things I cannot abide
Life will be brimming with new adventures galore
And I will never again let depression darken my door
Three cheers for the light that has shown me the way
And is hopefully now at last here to stay
It's a light that is hope and salvation in one
Illuminating the journey that I am now on!

Jason

When the passage of time calls out your name
And you know that nothing will ever be the same
Its then that you realise you are about to depart
As the last breath of air calms your beating heart
No more to be free to roam about at will
Your soul must depart and your body be still
Your journey has ended for the time being this day
Inevitable that we all have to pass through this way
Somehow I knew you were going to die
But never had the courage to say goodbye
I'm saying it now in the hope that you find
Yourself being remembered by those left behind
No one deserves to die it's an unwelcome event
Nature's way of saying that your body is spent
But your soul if you believe it can linger on
Forever in the courtyards of the holy one
In the house of the Lord a place exists
For everyone who believes that it's not to be missed
The Bible says three score years and ten
Are given as a down-payment to mortal men
There is a life hereafter promised to all
Who have repented their sins and have heeded the call
So let's not be hasty about dying in vain
If you love life don't treat your death with distain
Accept that your journey is a wonderous thing
And enjoy what you have and what it may bring
A means to an end it certainly is not
It's precious and it's the only one that you've got
If you feel like crying go ahead and cry
It's not often you see a life just sail by
But I prefer to give thanks for the day
When your suffering was ended and your soul flew away!

My Father

I found myself thinking about an old friend yesterday
Old enough to have disappeared and quietly flown away
He was a bastion of wisdom a tower of worldly strength
That's what I thought when I thought of him at length
It only occurred to me recently you see
That when I looked I could see a lot of him in me
I've grown to like him now that I am getting old
Mindful of his ways and remembering what I was told
My father loved me like a candle to a flame
Flooding light into the night and taking all the blame
His eyes would sparkle at the mention of my name
Forever a beacon in life's unfolding game
A father needs a son like an oak tree needs wood
To grow and to nurture into something very good
My father fashioned me with the care and patience of Job
Gifting me with lessons from his own treasure trove
I loved him with humility and he loved me back
Trundling along on life's railway track
A journey that would last from the day that I was born
Until the day that he vanished and an angel was born
I don't know if he is in the company of St Peter or St Paul
But I do know that he is missed by us all
I say silent prayers for a life that ended too fast
Like a shooting star whose track does not last
When a son's father dies the earth weeps blood
Cleansed only by prayers to the Almighty up above
Leaving behind garlands of flowers in the ground
Like a blanket of roses waiting to be found!

My Mother

The memories of you come to a blind man at dawn
A sweet endless tune since the day that I was born
The music of life has a powerful beat
You had that and now you have made your retreat
I listen for echoes of you every day
It's been so long now since you went away
I loved you so much that my life fell apart
But now I am listening to the sound of my heart
I lost sight of you but now the memories are strong
I'm building the pictures and it won't be long
Before I can open my eyes and once again see
The images of you in a reflection of me
I'm a man on a mission with a will to survive
Intent on keeping our close feelings alive
It takes time to recover from the loss of a friend
But I am sure now that my heart will soon mend!

Tragedy

If the chemistry of life includes love I want to know why
Acorns can fall to the ground and then reach to the sky
If men and women find that love does not last
Is it a mistake to think about the past
It was as if a piece of the jigsaw was wrong
So I found a new piece that made me feel strong
My first love went off with a stranger who promised to be
More understanding of her deeper needs than me
That's what happened and I remember it well
Though I have to admit I fell under the spell
Of the need to use alcohol to extinguish the flame
Of what had gone wrong and take most of the blame
The smouldering bonfire of my life had been seen
For what it was and what it had been
By another acorn that wanted to be
As proud as an oak with some help from me
The balance of my life changed the moment I said
I want to embrace another instead
I loved my acorn and she made me feel love
For the first time in a long time I had a turtle dove
The intensity of the bond was as strong as I had known
Reinforcing itself with the love that was shown
How was I to know that it would reluctantly melt
Under the strain of the pressures we both felt
The last time I saw her was when I flew to Kuwait
I wrote her a letter saying I loved her too late
When I came back to face the music I felt the despair
Of two loves blown away and vanishing into thin air!

The Waiting Room

What puzzles me now is what to do
My questions are many but the answers are few
What is happening to me is a mystery so deep
That I struggle to find solace even in sleep
The long days and nights merge and I soldier on
Like a candle with no flame whose bright light has gone
I am only a shadow whose torch is now cold
Frightened of dying as I become old
One day soon I will take my last breath
Close my eyes firmly and experience death
It will come to us all I know that for sure
A final farewell that we have to endure
A phantom will come wearing a mask
And ask me for payment to complete his task
His task is to ferry my soul to a place
Where the rivers run dry and you may not hide your face
The inquisitor will ask questions and look into my eyes
Reaching in to discover the depths of my lies
Only if the blemishes can be removed with a prayer
Will he ever allow me to move on from there
And move on I must if I don't want to take blame
For the years spent in limbo living with shame
I know all this because my life was a lie
Too often in the balance when I was ready to die
I threw away the key to the door through which men go
If they don't have a dice that they are willing to throw
Like a chalice emptying itself through a crack
Made by Satan himself through which you can never look back
The cocktail which I drank that almost killed me
Was a brew so potent that I will never be free
Unless of course the prayers I have made
Remove the shackles that bind me causing me to fade
Only then will I recover my life's inner spark
And burn brightly once more to see through the dark
I'm looking for forgiveness or salvation at best
So that my last mortal remains can be laid firmly to rest
Thereby allowing my soul the chance to live on
In the kingdom of heaven where I would like to belong
What puzzles me now is what to do
My questions are many but the answers are few

Bridgette the Bicycle

It was unfair to criticise Bridgette that way
It was my fault she was in the saddle that day
Her friends or her enemies were just having some fun
So they wrote in the rag mag that's how it was done
I wasn't too impressed with the phrase "Tallyho"
Attributed to me for letting myself go
With an attractive female student up for the chance
To make love to me and start a romance
Bridgette read literature and took an interest in men
She stood out from the crowd before she was ten
I fell in love with her the moment she said
"I'm sure we've met before" and it was straight off to bed.
She was bright as a button and funny as well
Good company for me and I fell under her spell
Monogamy was anathema to Bridgette at first
She had every right to play the field first
It didn't take long for word to get around
And her friends were jealous of what she had found
A kindred spirit with similar interests and a spark
To ignite fires in the belly and ignore the dark
Bridgette was pragmatic sensible and good
And I gave her my heart like no one else could
She in turn loved me as much as she could love
Burning up our passions like a bonfire burns wood
I can honestly say that when push comes to shove
I am wedded to her memory and frankly still in love
I would like to meet her again and show respect
Honouring each other never to neglect
Spontaneous to a fault I'll lay my feelings bare
And willingly salute her just for being there!

Abandoned

Like a blanket of rain from which nothing can run
The shadow of you shuts out the sun
You left me in darkness without much ado
Leaving your footprints behind just like a burglar would do
The heavens opened and the storm clouds appeared
Like the woollen-coats of black sheep being sheared
A bubbling cauldron stirred up in the sky
Overflowing to wash away the disbelief in my eye
Black sheep are totally distinct from the flock
As a panel of jurors is from the accused in the dock
With your finger pointing you cloaked me in rain
I had no warning no note to explain
Begging the question why on earth did I try
To share my whole life with you by living a lie
It took many a dark day and night in retreat
To think things through and finally conquer defeat
After that my thoughts became clear
Only then did I know I had nothing to fear
Like a sacrificial lamb I was offered up to take blame
As the reason you were unfaithful and living with shame
I was never the reason behind that as you know
As always you just didn't know how far to go
Better that you now live in the company of a thief
Who stole my pride for a while and caused me such grief
That way you can suffer agonies untold
When you both live with your guilt as you grow old
Abandoning all that you ever held dear
Struck me at the time as being wholly insincere
You left behind the rock on which you were built
And got carried away by a river of silt
Dark stories misrepresentations and lies
Are not the only things I discovered about your disguise
I searched my heart every day for what seemed like a year
Until I was happy that my recalcitrance was clear
Only then did I finally commit
To freeing myself from the bondage and shackles remit
That you placed on me when you decided to smite me
With the Cheshire cat's smile which you used to bite me

I finally realised with counselling from people in the know
That the best thing to do was to just let you go
I'm happy now that I have conquered the demon in my life
To carry on without you causing any more strife
I must admit that you had me fooled for years
But I look forward now to a life without tears!

The Tree of Life!

To settle a legitimate grievance with life
It's better to not consider using a knife
To end your own life with the thrust of a blade
Is like cutting the tree from which you are made
No acorns will fall from your oak anymore
And your branches will wither and fall to the floor
The leaves that were once so distinctive to see
Will scatter in the wind and no longer be
Able to sustain the life that you had
Be it good indifferent tragic or sad
An acorn is worthy of life from the start
So why when we are trees do we sometimes lose heart
Is it because we are embarrassed to say
That life has gone wrong and we don't like it that way
If the future is suggesting that the weather may be
About to turn nasty and uproot the tree
Maybe it's better to anticipate what will come
And think very carefully about what can be done
I think that when I tried to take my own life
Being frightened of old age with a large kitchen knife
I was mistakenly trying to remove the dead wood
That accumulates when times are not very good
I wanted to be proud perfect and free
Standing tall and unblemished for all to see
But the cancer of old age that will come to us all
Inevitably says we are all destined to fall
My judgement was clouded by depression at the time
But now that has gone and I'm feeling fine
Experience has taught me that it's better to try
Again and again and again not to cry
Grow old gracefully and accept what you get
From the tree of life and never forget
If the problems you are facing are getting you down
Don't waste your acorns and continue to frown
Be positive be industrious be busy and let's see
If you can change your mind about suicide like me
An acorn can be an idea in your head
Which you can ruminate on before you go to bed
Pretty soon one day you will find
The acorn has grown and has filled your mind
With a forest of possibilities on how to explore

The world that exists outside of your door
Don't let suicide tempt you to end
A life which is precious and can easily mend
If you believe in where there's a will there's a way
Promise yourself never to do it today
I have no grievance with life anymore
Although I am aware that I knocked on death's door
What's changed for me I can't really say
Except to say that I am now thinking this way
You could say that I have learned the lesson for good
That a tree is a tree and a wood is just wood
But the magic in me that my acorn contained
Is still bursting with life and forever remains
Thankfully rooted to life's holy grail
For anyone like me who lives to tell the tale
It's now ingrained in my conscience to refrain
And not to needlessly take my own life in vain
I am now content to stand proud in the wood
Because my acorn has grown wise and lives on like it should!

The Marie Celeste

If ever a ship knew the depths of despair
And could fathom the hearts of men who had died there
It's the Marie Celeste for aimlessly roaming the seas
With no hope, no life and alone in the breeze
I liken myself to the Marie Celeste
Because my mother has died and is now at rest
Her soul was set free from an ocean full of pain
But is now safe in a harbour where peace will remain
When a ship has no crew and a prevailing wind blows
It doesn't know better than to go where it goes
A rudderless ship is a strange thing indeed
Not what you want in your hour of peril or great need
I am at the mercy of currents heralding death's door
No one at the rudder to help me ashore
Whither to steer port starboard or straight
Or just drift around in a figure of eight
A gold Spanish doubloon that was nailed to the mast
Now the only thing to remind the ship of the past
It's Davy Jones' locker for a crew now at rest
For them to believe it was lucky a tall story at best
The voices still echo around the lonely decks
Awash with the pain of years of neglect
The creaks and the groans from the men and the ship
Still appear to be somehow joined at the hip
Possessed now with cries from an albatross host
Who has dared to follow in the wake of the ghost
It's unlikely that the bird will find anything to do
As the Marie Celeste is without a crew
One of the deepest and greatest mysteries of all
Is to sail the seven seas and then take a sudden fall
Not to be seen after the ship gives up the race
And all souls aboard sink without a trace
But I believe if you can listen with great care
You will be lucky and find your albatross there
It's waiting for you before you abandon the ghost
Of your own ship forever and drown just like most
To the souls who spend most of their lost lives at sea
Never to be seen again possibly just like me
I say rise up listen and heed the albatross' call
It beckons to a change in the wind for us all
If I am the ship and the bird takes my soul

Flying away there is hope for us all
My soul will not die though the ship may well sink
And I will be saved forevermore to think
With so many questions and so little to do
Will I end up dying the same way as you
Believing that a loved one has cared until the last
Like that gold doubloon which is still nailed to the mast
My ship though for now continues to steer
By following the wind from here to here
Navigating life by God's good fortune at best
At the mercy of reefs and enduring every test
Whether I finally drop anchor or am smashed by the sea
Largely depends on my willingness to be
The author of my own destiny in this tragedy today
A ship in a bottle if you want to look at it that way
It's a mystery to me why the Marie Celeste
Doesn't just sink and be done with the past
That way we would all be entitled to pray
For the many lost souls wandering to this day
To salvage the shell of a ship doomed to die
Rather than to just let flotsam drift by
Would be a blessing in disguise for all those in hell
Suffering in silence without a ship's bell
So let's hope that when the ghost ship is found
Long before she flounders or finally runs aground
I am saved and can chart a new route to a place
Where I am reunited with my mother's tranquil face
I can resurrect all the feelings I had
When my mother was alive and times were not bad
I deserve better than to live here like a ghost
So as God is my witness I will do my upmost
A ship's biscuit is what I will have with some tea
When I remember the good times had by my mother and me
Both rescued from the depths of despair
By an Albatross who mysteriously appeared out of thin air!

One Too Many

A philosopher's knot is what my head is now in
Looking for a place to forgive myself sin
A place to untie my psyche and think
What happened to me when I started to drink
I have all the right words and I'm in the frame of mind
To write the story of my life without being unkind
So here goes to first line first chapter first verse
This is for real no more time to rehearse.
Gone is the reason to drink from my life
Removed with the precision of a scalpel or knife
Not without some hesitation or pain
I am telling the truth about loss love and pain
If ever a man needed a bulletproof vest
It's me for what I am about to get off my chest
My journey has been tortuous valiant and just
A testimony to a battle with overindulgence if you must
When you need a drop of alcohol to fathom the deep
Of the trouble you are in without any sleep
You have crossed the Rubicon just like I did
Without realising it will cost you more than just a few quid
To drink to excess and spend all your money
Is seldom successful and not at all funny
Your hopes and ambitions vanish in the flash of an eye
And you can kiss a life of sobriety goodbye.
The cause of my drinking was depression and stress
I overplayed my cards and drank to excess
Not thinking that I would lose control of the plot
To stay in control and lose everything I'd got
I also took full blame for something I felt
The loss of a loved one that gave me a belt
My body went numb and I drank every day
To anaesthetise myself and take the pain away
How you may ask did I arrive at the place
Where sanity and reason replaced the disgrace
Of needing to feed the greed of a thing
As dangerous as addiction and what that may bring
I simply decided to not touch a drop
As the only way for the nightmare to stop
It's working for me and my life is on track
To get all my self-esteem and self-confidence back
It's really amazing how your concentration improves

When you have solemnly pledged to give up the booze
To be bright as a button is what you notice first
Free from the blindfold with which you were cursed
To be truly abstinent is to light up your spark
For the good things in life and emerge from the dark
You discover you are capable of living with your past
And looking forward to the future at last
A good song becomes a breath of fresh air
To blow away the cobwebs and every trace of despair
The music of life returns with a beat
Heralding your return from the depths of defeat
In short once you have made up your mind
That you will never drink alcohol remember to be kind
To yourself first of all for having had the good sense
To accept the challenge and come down off the fence
Remember that one too many is a road to despair
To recover from alcohol is usually quite rare
It's the first drink that is the downfall of all
So don't have one and you can be sure to stand tall
I now consider myself to be unshackled and free
From the demons inside that were consuming me
Gone is the need to fuel the thirst for a drink
I have succeeded in pulling myself back from the brink
Sobriety gives me another reason to think
How good life can be when you don't need to drink
Never again to be burdened with desires
Which dampen your spirit and put out your fires
You can once again sparkle as nature intended
And turn a blind eye to the day you offended
Yourself by choosing to obliterate your woes
With the cocktail of poison you unwittingly chose
These days it's not hard for me to understand why
I was so deeply depressed that I wanted to die
Now the only thing left of the demon inside
Is the ghost of my past which I cannot abide!

Hypnos

I fell asleep not knowing if I would die
Whilst an anaesthetist kept a watchful eye
His main concern was to try to save my life
A tragedy in the making if it didn't go right
A surgical team had been assembled straight away
When I presented with a knife wound on that fateful day
I had mistakenly thought that they would never succeed
In saving my life in my hour of great need
What prompted me to try to run myself through
Was the fear of old age and having nothing to do
Also I had nursed my mother with a terminal disease
An effort on my part which brought me to my knees
She died in the grip of the most terrible pain
Which surged through her body time and time again
It was only when morphine cocktails were pumped in through her veins
That her spirit departed and left behind her remains
The shock that I felt when she left me behind
Was enough to shake and unbalance my state of mind
So the thought of joining her finally at peace
Drove me to contemplate my own release
I reasoned incorrectly that God had no place
At the table of remembrance where I hid my sad face
My last meal was too difficult to swallow
It was the realisation that there would be no tomorrow
It took me 4 hours to summon the strength
To push in the knife all nine inches in length
I didn't feel any pain at all
So nine is my lucky number after all
The ambulance crew that came from nearby
After I changed my mind and didn't want to die
Were heroes to get me to the theatre in time
For the surgery that eventually made me feel fine.
To owe a debt of gratitude is not a bad thing
When you think of the situation that you were in
So I write to the surgeon occasionally to say
Thank you for what you did on that day
My life was saved and now I take great pride
In my physical and mental health having almost died
I will live in Elysium for a thousand years or more
And challenge Methuselah to be last through deaths door
I sleep like a baby with one eye open at night

Only to peek and see if the light
Is enough to wake me from the dream that I dream
Which is to one day eat strawberries and cream
That was the treat that my mother and I
Would sometimes eat after a home-made meat pie
I pray for her at least once everyday
And promise never to take my own life come what may!

Judgement Day

It showed in Christ's eyes that are saddened by pain
As he summoned up the strength to cry out his name
Revealing himself at the dawn of man to be
The Saviour from the Sea of Galilee
On the day of reckoning its written in a book
That mortal men will be witness to the day the Earth shook
Praying themselves that Jesus will show the way
By proclaiming to the Almighty that he is the Christ on that day
According to many clues are now only to be found
Written on pages buried out of sight in consecrated ground
The way to navigate stars the naked heavens hold
Is to light up the sky with candles burning cold
If the meaning of life is in question now
So is the thirst for knowledge somehow
Sought by the ones who earnestly pray
For the right to forgiveness on judgement day
So it is, within the hearts of men
Respecting all the commandments ten
Lost in space with nowhere to go
Until they are driven mad and buried in snow
Seeking shelter warmth and love
They mistakenly pray to their God above
Asking for the Earth to split asunder
With raging storms and peels of thunder
Better to know that in the depths of a prayer
Angels can appear and light the way there
Illuminating the pathway which the Lord has prepared
In order that their lives can finally be spared
Genesis tore down the walls of shame
So that mortal men could in freedom reign
Supreme on the Earth as guardians of trust
Abandoning the need for avarice and lust
Born to live and fight Satan's will
Swallowing their pride like a bitter pill
Brave men walk over the graves of fear
Instilled in them by his presence here
Certain in the knowledge that come what may
When the Almighty saves the Earth one day
The wheels of fortune will spell out his name
When asked to turn back the tides of shame
If the Almighty can take the time to do all this

Sealing our fate with a loving kiss
Isn't it time that Jehovah was seen
In the footsteps of time where mortal men have been
I give thanks to the Lord from my tower every day
Asking for forgiveness when I start to pray
Recognising his face in every line soaked in blood
Crucified and nailed to a cross made of wood!

The Submariner

A man from under the sea said to me
I do it as a means to an end for a fee
A Submariner is what they call me at home
A rover blessed with the freedom to roam
Unfettered by chains to the land or the air
I breathe an artificial climate down there
Germ free unpolluted and clean
A laboratory for men to work in and dream
Once I dive down to the depths of the sea
The atmosphere dictates the person I'll be
With a captain in charge of running the boat
The crew works together to keep us afloat
As an instrument of war a submarine has no peer
Built to attack and intimidate with fear
Striking at targets within reach on dry land
If ordered to by the fleet's high command
Like a scorpion with a venomous sting
The submarine can strike at any living thing
In pursuit of a way to prevent war
It can obliterate the threats until they are threatening no more
Self-gratification and the endless quest for power
Locks some men's hearts into an ivory tower
Leading them to follow sinful ways that arise
Deep within their psyche behind lying eyes
A submarine can perform an operation so deep
That these men's ambitions are put straight to sleep
Never again to upset the balance of power
Preserved very delicately like an inert dried flower
He said he wouldn't swop the isolation the depths bring
For being lost in a crowded park in the spring
Because such is the draw of the mysteries of the deep
That he felt comfortable in his artificial retreat
I got the feeling when I looked into his watery eyes
That he had been awake for an eternity and had severed his ties
With relationships that lead to a grave full of dust
Compromised by iron clad feelings that inevitably rust
Solitude at sea is the fulcrum of life
Pitching this way and that through your troubles and strife
Better to play out an order to submerge
Than to remain aloof when you get the urge
To follow orders is to denigrate the freedom to think

A bit like agreeing to eat sleep or drink
For someone who doesn't like authority to wear
The cloak of an acquiescent murderer down there
A submariner deserves respect it must be said
For patrolling the minefields of the living dead
That's how I choose to think of his career
A sacrifice to preserve the things we hold dear!

Life's Like That

If you don't know the difference between right and wrong
How can your moral fibre carry you along
To not know which foot to put forward first
Is like walking the tightrope with which you are cursed

Better to think carefully before you tumble and fall
Like an acrobat trying to make sense of it all
You have to be in tune with yourself to succeed
So move step by step and just do what you need

Don't rush or make haste in this world full of woe
It's cold unforgiving and cruel not to know
The right way to solve the problems that you face
Or to conquer your demons in the first place

That takes planning insight and valour
Coupled with a non-judgemental manner
Qualities you may just have in reserve
If you can quietly and carefully summon up the nerve

When faced with a problem take one step back
A good solid defence is better than attack
If you commit only to that which you believe to be right
Darkness will lift and be replaced by the light!

One Day You'll Fly Away

One day soon you'll up and fly away
I know this because not even robins come to stay
You'll get the urge to let your wings unfold
And leave once again making my blood run cold

You'll fly at night and navigate by the stars
To the sound of mandolins and rhythmic guitars
On the trail to hide in some secret place
Like a thief who has recently fallen from grace

Loves labours lost will be your reward
For the time you spent collecting your hoard
Like a Wall Street banker you will take the cash
And turn my dreams into a pile of smoke and ash

Although my life will never quite be the same
I will like a phoenix rise from what remains
To build another life having finally learned to cope
With tragedies no matter how distant or remote

Such is the fleeting promise of a house built of wood
Fashioned to cradle all the promises of good
Times to be had if I believed what you say
About love and trust and judgement day

Oh to bite the apple without breaking a heart
Or to plant a seed and let it grow in the dark
What good is a promise if it cannot fulfil
Like the myth of Sisyphus rolling a stone up a hill

When you pray to an angel to grant you a wish
Or shoot at a target and hope not to miss
Let the arrow from loves bow find its own way
To the one true love you hope to meet one day

If you meet that love grab it with both hands
And put into place some elaborate plans
Hide it away deep in the maze of your heart
So that it can always remain and never depart!

The Mind of God

It needs no more than a whisper to God
To make even the mundane seem odd
If you want to change water into wine
You will not be the first to be that way inclined

Like Isaac Newton watching the fate of the apple
To understand the gravity of the laws which he grappled
Or Adam facing the consequences of taking the fruit
Seeing it fall into his hands and thinking it was loot

Our lives are governed by the arrow of time
Shot from the crossbow of the heavens divine
We are measured by the illuminating arc of its trace
As if falls to Earth with good-natured grace

If your whisper is no more than a soft gentle breeze
Picked up by the Almighty with consummate ease
He will grant you an audience with that which you need
The council of the Mind of God on which you may feed

The Mind of God can manoeuvre steer and replenish
The facts of your being until you have finished
Exhausting the fabric of your God-given right
To understand everything about your own plight

If stone can be raised to fashion a temple
And grinding a mountain to dust is as simple
I challenge my God to set me a task
And remain at his mercy for as long as it lasts

I pray to touch the fabric of time
And feel the embrace of all that's divine
To glow on the cusp of a furnace burning like gold
Never to fail as I live and grow old

The Mind of God fathoms the dominions of men
As surely as floods once completely covered them
An ocean of teardrops shed in the blink of an eye
To wash away evil without needing to cry

The Mind of God is at work on the Earth
As witnessed by the arrival of every new birth
The new sparks that ignite are produced from thin air
A testament to his involvement there

The Mind of God is omnipotent it seems
And may even permeate dreams
A guardian of all that is thought to be known
About the way we think when we are alone

I think therefore I am a good place to start
A beginning to understanding the heart
If your heart is true and your thinking is clear
You are on the right path and your destiny is near

But what price a man alone in a field
With no harvest to gather and ground that will not yield
Or a man who needs water but cannot make bread
What then, what then can be said

If it is easier for a camel to pass through a crack in a wall
Than for a rich man to enter the Kingdom of Heaven at all
Surely a poor man with no water or bread
Can take the place of the rich man instead

If I enter myself through a crack in the wall
Can I know the fate of my soul
I am curious to find an oasis in there
For the ship of my desert which is also laid bare

The Mind of God governs all that we know
When we are lost in the wilderness with nowhere to go
So I come to you as a supplicant would
Asking you the right way to go as I should!

The Rain

Rain covered the pavement like the dew on a leaf
Caressing it as softly as a kiss from a thief
Stolen when the victim was soundly asleep
And leaving an imprint but not very deep

More of a mist than raindrops falling free
It felt like a damp cloak wrapped around me
The rain carried on for a brief spell at most
Conjuring up at times the shadows of ghosts

All this whilst the early morning light
Shone through the cracks in a vanishing night
Like the fingers of fortune on a wheel of roulette
Spinning slowly to reveal what sort of day we will get

Not knowing whether to be still or be blown
The wind was locked out until the wheel's final turn
Waiting patiently to match the strength and the need
To the wheel when shown the direction and speed

As time moved on the day broke with a sigh
Releasing more rain from the eyes in the sky
Teardrops fashioned to wash away the sleep
And blanket the ground after slumbers so deep

The mists became brooks and the brooks became streams
The streams ran together and created oceans it seems
Soon the pavements were awash with the tide
Of the rain as it looked for somewhere to hide

Finding drains at the side of the road
Rivulets ran underground to ease the wet load
Leaving the pavements glistening wet
The roulette wheel having paid out on its bet

Some people say you can smell rain in the air
And predict when it's on its way from its lair
A fresh smell as fresh as the day that it greets
When it finally falls and intoxicates our streets

It's the liquor of life on which all things depend
To exist in this world and not ultimately spend
Time soaking up rain like a prune in the sun
Unrecognisable unless the rains work is done

You can be driven mad by rain if the wind is just right
Howling and fashioning pitter patters in the night
Sometimes it doesn't just rain it pours
Like silver threads being woven outdoors

Where it all goes to is anybody's guess
But we all think we could do with a lot less
Until we face drought which is frightening indeed
Requiring conservation and the planting of seed

Rain could be considered to be God's gift from the sky
In pharaohs' time when the planting of seed crops was nigh
Raising the Nile to flood alluvial plains
In order to produce the necessary grains

Without rain the earth would be dormant and dry
Withering away until the new crops just die
With rain the harvests are an expectant return
Like meeting an old friend for whom your candles still burn

I don't know why rain gets such a bad name
Unless it's because we need something to blame
For the way we are feeling on a particular day
Getting caught out in a downpour and wishing it away

Rain is to an old man a reason to live
Watering his desires and inspiring him to give
Credence to the notion that a flower will grow
For every good deed he has managed to sow

Rain is to a young man a reminder to make
Allowances for every single mistake
That he as an old man will want to put right
Washing his conscience clean in the depths of the night

Rain is the vehicle of water on the move
Forever advancing like a tyre in a groove
Driving forward the Circle of Life at a pace
Like the never-ending threads in a garment of lace

If ever the rain could speak its own name
It would say nothing except from Zeus that it came
The father of the Gods has fashioned it well
When the rain falls we are firmly under its spell!

The Final Curtain

My mother died today or was it yesterday
I'd never seen flesh stretch out on bones and then just fade away
It took 10 days to melt her will and break the spirit too
I watched intently not sleeping there was nothing else to do

Death wears no mask and I wish with all my heart
That I could have avoided that particular part
The face she left behind was not the one I knew
It was agony it was pain and it was almost turning blue

When we die we simply cease to be
That which we were or were shortly meant to be
Time stops and in one second a candles flame goes out
Vanishing into space that we never talk about

Immortality is the time it takes to register your name
On the list of volunteers who would like to do the same
It's a wishing well you need to throw the completed list into
So that posterity will do unto others as they do unto you

To be remembered famously is an ambition and a goal
If you are insecure enough to want to do it at all
Enlightenment is for those who for some reason are not
Content to appreciate themselves for that which they've got

As I had watched my mother's life just ebb and flow away
Like an iceberg melting a little every day that followed day
The morphine pumps were busy managing the pain
And I wanted desperately to try to do the same

The ice-cold facts of life are in a mortuary fridge
Nonetheless to have lived at all is a privilege
The warmth of your birth and the life that you lead
Is testament to your hearts ability to bleed

Our feelings about death are often hidden from view
Behind the final curtain so we don't know what to do
When a loved one dies and leaves us in distress
Struck by grief feeling numb and that sense of worthlessness

Exhaustion beckoned as they took her corpse away
I needed sleep and rest to fight another day
She meant the world to me and I would miss her from the start
Now behind the final curtain and forever in my heart

Death is the chopping block of a butcher's trade in meat
Returning that which was alive to be sold for money in the street
If I had an axe to grind I would ask him to wield it once for me
And cut off the pain of dying from all humanity!

A Leprechaun's Tale

If I could untie a philosopher's knot
And put rhyme before reason what have I got
A tale I can tell without worrying about meaning
And concentrate on which way the story is leaning

I would tell you the tale of a leprechaun's delight
In hiding his gold and counting it all night
Only to discover at the break of day
That one gold piece was missing and had melted away

It seems that the more you count on it the less you have got
A familiar tale to those who have and have not
At a loss to explain how more becomes less
Before we find ourselves in a bit of a mess

A leprechaun is a fortunate fellow indeed
To hide gold at the end of a rainbow and not need
To worry about anybody seeing it there
After daylight has come and it vanishes into thin air

It cannot be approached in the cold light of day
And a leprechaun is reluctant to give it away
It is not a recklessly extravagant resource
But it does have a useful purpose of course

Leprechauns do trades if you're willing to believe
That a story is worth money if not meant to deceive
So tell him a tale and see what you get
A mischievous wink and a gold coin for a bet

He will bet you that he has heard if before
And that it is already part of Irish folklore
In which case you will have to forfeit your bet
And pay him before you get into debt

When they say that the Irish are rich in folklore
And the luck of the Irish brings money to their door
Spare a thought for the way you were charmed out of gold
By a Leprechauns tale and the way it was told!

New York

Skyscrapers are the American way
Loud ostentatious and lit up night and day
Elevators to take you up and people to let you down
Buildings to tell a tale like Liberty and her Crown

The Empire State building is now a needle in the hay
A wheat field of dreams on a sunlit New York day
A harvest of men's ideas on how to tame a field
With steel glass and concrete and build them for real

Millions of windows and millions of views
Each one inviting and exciting people to choose
The one to your liking and the one that will not do
Expressing themselves as only Americans do

I wouldn't say I don't like the American way
Or the things that Americans get away with when they pray
I would just say that on occasion it's a lot to take in
For God to bless America and then to free it from sin

New York is a haven for business to flourish and thrive
With Wall Street in the centre bringing it alive
It's a cornucopia of industrious reward
A tribute to the misers and those who can hoard

With alleyways at the bottom and penthouses at the top
There's somewhere for everyone to sleep when they drop
The way up is long and the fall down is fast
Should your dollar bills desert you and you're down to the last

The city runs on money like an engine needs its oil
With people spending it like water in their daily toil
Millionaires abound but are much fewer in number
Than those who work harder before they can slumber

The city that never sleeps is finding it hard to compete
With Maine or uptown areas that offer a quiet retreat
If you persist in constantly depriving yourself of sleep
It will not be long before you are buried six feet deep

People love New York as an exciting location
To visit and be intoxicated on a thrill seeking vacation
But like sunshine if you stay out in it you can expect
To get burned and dried up like a victim of neglect

To live in New York you have to be accustomed to greed
Making money a priority to satisfy needs
Only then can you relax at the end of the day
And maybe for good measure stash a little bit away

I like New York not because its brash
Loud and vulgar or on occasion quite flash
I like it because it's fashioned from the toil
Of the millions whose ideas have been brought it to the boil

If you sit on a park bench and think of the Freedom Tower
You won't be the first to spend a New York hour
Marvelling at what has been achieved
It has to be seen to be believed!

Love Is

Love is like a bridge that takes you far away
From loneliness and isolation every single day
Love can treat and cure feelings as remote
As disappointment and apathy like a magic antidote

Love can level playing fields that once were worn and torn
To give you time to build the future like a seeded watered lawn
Love is the feeling you get from ignoring the Spartan way
And accepting a Trojan horse as an apology each day

There are many ways to fill your heart with love
But I think that the easiest is to pray to your God above
If you can do that and satiate your need
You can drink loves potion deep and invigorate your seed

You will have no need for the darker things that tempt you astray
And you can share in your loves labours every single day
Love can be as gentle as dew settling on a lily's curled-up flower
Or as invigorating as the onset of an April thunderstorm or shower

When two people share the bonds of earthly love
They are inviting in a lifetime of blessings from above
Only if you give love can you know what it's like to kneel and pray
And never die of thirst in a desert far away!

Life on Mars

I'd like to go to Mars and see
The watching stars as the stars see me
A speck of light in heavens eye
A teardrop burning in the sky

The stars pinned out across the sky
Like the rubies in a tiger's eye
Would gaze at me and hold my glare
Surprised to even find me there

Floating free but held in space
The myriad of stars resembles lace
Spun from the cosmic threads of time
And somehow crocheted by hooks divine

My face covered with the soft embrace
Of the patterns embedded in the lace
I could peep through keyholes to look and see
If anyone was looking back at me

When life on the earth had just begun
Mars was forth in line to the sun
Barren except for gods it seems
That wage war in clouds of steam

Why on Earth and not on Mars
A cupid's arrow shot from the stars
Forever targeting the Earth to be
A lifeboat in loves geometry

The red planets cloak of sterile rust
Hides a war of interplanetary dusts
Bombarded and deep cratered skin
Now conceals the spoils within

The moons of Mars were captured when
Two asteroids ventured to move in
Too close not to be casualties of war
Not too far from the Earths front door

If we can send an envoy to Mars
A lifeboat to explore the stars
I would venture to abandon ship
And man the lifeboat to conquer it

The Clockmaker

A clockmaker watches the time everyday
As the seconds become minutes and the hours tick away
Building a future from designs that were drawn
Long ago by stargazers copying their movements till dawn

Painstakingly assembling wheels gears and parts
Revolving and ultimately resembling the heart
Beating in tune with nature and the seasons
A triumphant march to a tune for good reasons

You can copy a masterpiece and a clock does that well
So that we don't have to look to nature to tell
When we need to do something as important as to feed
The arrow of time with the planting of seed

A clock can get wound up if you don't treat it well
Giving you no time at all as far as I can tell
Causing an alarm to ring out as a surprise
To see the time you have set with your own eyes

A clock has a duty to soldier on to the last
Marching in time with the drums of the past
Advancing with every step every day
Napoleon sacrificed an army to make it that way

A clock is a precision instrument at times
Stretching the imaginary lines
Of what human beings can achieve when they try
To engineer ways to say hello and goodbye

A clock is also a work of art
Fashioned by an artist alone in the dark
Waiting for someone to show him the way
To be valued for what he has done every day

Some say that the Gods are at work in a clock
Fashioning miracles for the many and those who have not
Realised that the passage of time goes one way
Offering some direction till your dying day

If you can love a clock you can pay homage to time
Especially if you believe in the water and the wine
I pray at the same time everyday
In the hope that my prayers are important today

A clock takes only from the future and not from the past
Having no memory of things that do not last
It's up to us to record as history in a book
The events that befall us and the time that they took

A clockmaker fashions a way to travel in time
And builds a monument to his life and the sublime
Once he is a master of his trade
Observing the intimate beauty of what he has made

I know a clockmaker who is seeking perfection
Fastidious multitalented and without predilection
His clocks are a wonder to own and to hold
A close connection with a man who has a heart of gold

A clock has a face and a key to unlock
A time to be happy and one when you're not
It all depends on just how you feel
And how lucky you are on life's fortune wheel!

Devil or No

When the devil wakes me at 3 in the morning to try
To see beyond my defences and seduce me with a lie
I am careful not to use profanities like he utters every day
But I am firm in my resolve that he should listen to what I say

Let the truth be the truth when I quietly sing
It's in the nature of every living thing
To be fashioned by a power stronger than yours
One that breathes clean air and inhabits distant shores

Black is the lie and white is the truth
Night is not day and stars are the roof
Of the Universe which does not gamble or spend
The currency of corruption to its own end

You are the embodiment of one who has spent
Too much time plotting to extract your own rent
With the money from the houses of people in need
You profiteer and follow the signpost to your own greed

If I had my way I would raise your house to the ground
And knock down your temple as you sleep safe and sound
Leaving no trace except a black hole in the ground
Into which I would throw the begging bowl I have found

When you next visit the wishing well which you have sunk
You may use the begging bowl to get quietly drunk
On your own power and you will now need to defend
The company you keep and the money that you spend

It's two steps forward and one step back
When I turn defence into attack
The move that will paralyse you before nightfall the next day
Will sicken you to the stomach as I pray

It's a monumental battle when enlisted to a cause
To raise up the stones and grasp the bloody rose
The thorns of the stems do not wither like the flower
To win a war you have to draw blood and defend an ivory tower

A real temple is not built with the chattels of a war
But from the stones that were once laid as a foundation to my door
My ivory tower will not crumble at the sight of every thief
Who tries to steal my opinions views and beliefs

I aligned myself with the Mormons some years ago
In a winter of discontent when I was covered in snow
The snow melted the day that they invited me in
To worship away any thoughts I may have that were conducive to sin

A Mormon has strength wisdom and faith
A depository of values to be kept sound and safe
Locked into the light and the fundamental way
Shining a torch into the vaults of the temple every day

A temple to a Mormon is an open book
Inviting readers to take a second look
At the coming of Christ and the future of mankind
A vision of clarity to those who were once blind!

I'm not entirely sure if I can live the Mormon way
So I content myself with my cocoon of virtue and try not to go astray
When I emerge to the sound of a distant bell
It will be because I have escaped the ravages of Hell

I feel heavy with a burden I do not understand
And the need for a patient friend to come and hold my hand
Whilst I tell him the story of how at last I found my way
To the sermon on the mount and began to pray

If for some reason I am not able
To furnish bread at my last supper's table
Or to meaningfully sip wine to welcome you in
Forgive me absolve my sin and cleanse me within

I wish to stand tall impeccable and just
So that I can face the devil and tell him that I trust
Not the devil in me or the devil in him
And watch him disappear behind his twisted sick beguiling grin

The devil inhabits places that you find
In the crevasses that an avalanche leaves behind
In the tortuously constructed labyrinth of your mind
It is necessary to uncover what you find

Burn him out with flares of elemental white
Shine a torch to extinguish all but light
Remove all traces of the threat to open wide
A chasm that will beckon at your side

Tread the path to your chosen one with care
Take the summit road and he will meet you there
To rejoice with him in the steps you have made
The Lord's Prayer will be your accolade!

The Fisherman

If I get lonely on occasion I have a cup of tea
Ignore it and wash away my vanity
Stay happy in the knowledge that eventually somebody will come
And break the silence before the long day is done

The monotonous tick of the clock on the wall
Reassuringly announces its presence to all
Who enter my inner sanctum by the open door
Through which those lost at sea come floating ashore

My company is a harbour or a seaman's retreat
For those tired of running away with the fleet
A place to stay true to the desires of their hearts
When the storms out there have assiduously torn them apart

The days of rum rations and convivial camaraderie
Were enough to make friends with the salty dogs of the sea
Each with a tale bigger than the last
Like the one that got away with the indiscretions of the past

When seamen risk everything by trusting a ship
That is rusty and leaking and full of dried spit
They talk to each other about their lives and their loves
With an honesty devoid of exaggeration but not lust

With a fair maiden apparently waiting in every port
Lovers abound and are considered fair sport
Fishermen are only true to the sea
And one another of course whenever needs be

Like a shoal of dead herring old fisherman stink
Of too much rum and dead flesh after sailing close to the brink
It's a hard life trying to make a catch every day
Which is why a salty dog behaves in this way

Driven mad by the vagaries of having two wives
A life spent like this can wreak havoc with their lives
Committed to trying to fathom the deep
With no place to go except to hide in their sleep!

My Nurse

A firework went off when I opened my eyes
The bonfire of my passions had not yet died
This shell holds a man with a story to tell
You have prevented my soul from descending to Hell

There is something about you which is quite rare
Non-judgemental and willing to care
You shine with a gift which is beautiful to see
As special as the fruit is to the tree

If I said that I had been lucky that would not be enough
It's a miracle I survived after life has been so rough
Please think of me as the gentlest of men
With no malice and no wish to do what I did again

At peace now that I have been saved from death
By the nearest of margins and the preservation of my breath
An apology every day is what I must give
For losing my direction and not wanting to live

I give you that now and I mean every word
No matter if others may think it's absurd
Thank you for caring I love you for what you are
The loveliest nurse I have seen here by far!

A Final Prayer

A million words do not convey
The fullness of my love today
For my orator and my guide
Through which my mercies and my pride

Arrived at one with poignant grace
And brought me to this peaceful place
I feel the presence on this day
Weeping through my bones as I pray

With the hanging sword of Damocles
You have brought me to my bended knees
And I wish with all my pregnant heart
That I could make a brand-new start

On the road to far off Bethlehem
Amongst the lucky chosen men
Who will witness in their own short time
The fruits of labour and the vine

Eyes will open tears will run
To see the beauty of your son
And witness also the wisdom of men
Who will come and come again

Paying reverence and laying down
Gifts and offerings on the ground
Speaking truths to be passed on
When all the light in the world has gone

One day someone will come and say
Suffer not and gently pray
To a man who can climb the walls of shame
With pride to replace all thoughts of blame

Recognise in his blood stained face
Your own precipitous fall from grace
And try to love when you are unsure
Because only true love will endure

To save myself before it is too late
And forever seal my humble fate
I choose to give you this small prayer
And acknowledge that you are there…

"When worlds collide and heavens split
And light of light doth now permit
The blood to run and flesh to grow
It's only then that we will know!"

That mercy is the way to wonder
As pride in you tears my heart asunder
There is nothing left but to say goodbye.
To that which will now wither and die

Forgetting nothing and accepting all
I bare my breathless lifeless soul
To be resurrected by your side
Now that all that was undone has died

The son begets the fathers money
From the mother's womb as sweet as honey
A payment made should a new life grow
From alpha to omega as we know

It is finally time to say goodbye.
And leave the world with a tear in my eye
Questions many answers few
Never doubt my love for you!

Lost to Me

It was on the day my mother died
Or was it yesterday I can't remember
I watched the blood drain from her eyes
Now it's a memory in late September!

My father's life was just the same
As morphine leaked into his brain
Through numerous patches on his skin
Attached to kill the pain within

When pain is magnified a thousand fold
As the body suffers when it gets old
And God's gift is the only thing we've got
Diamorphine helps to hit the spot

It's harder than you think to end a life this way
With drugs that numb the senses everyday
But you can't deny a person's right
To choose this way to end the fight

I was skin and bone when I watched all this
Frightened to think that I would miss
The few remaining moments left to hold
The ones I loved dearly as they grew cold

A chill that makes you shiver accompanies the death
Impossible not to notice the stillness of the breath
Frozen in time like a camera which does not lie
Recording the agony of the moment when you die

The abyss doesn't open straight away
It waits until the soul departs and gently flies away
It's only then that you can see the manacles and the chains
That held together the fragments that remained

You bind yourself with those because that is all you know
A truth so cold it is like the driven snow
A snow which will bury the contours of your face
And hide the pain and suffering like a piece of crocheted lace

As the fog of time descends to depths as yet unknown
You realise that you are only flesh and bone
Wrapped in feelings which are bleeding from your heart
Like the drops of dew when each new day begins its careful start

The feelings depend largely on how you interpret grief
Robbing you of something special like an apocalyptic thief
The sense of loss is overpowering with its scale
Causing some who are not strong to suffer weep and wail

A wall exists to pass such feelings on
Near the birthplace of the Holy One
It costs nothing to give thanks and offer prayer
And hope that they are witness to you being there

If your only walls are the prison of what you thought
About them before they died your prayers will amount to nought
You must pray for them to be guided along the way
To their destiny with Saint Christopher before judgement day

Hopefully he will steer them blindly through the gates
To follow the path to righteousness and other heavenly fates
Only once their journey is complete
Will you return to a semblance of understanding where to meet

The ones you wished had never gone away
On the journey of a lifetime to be seen another day
Light of light truth of truth and the way to combat sin
I place my faith in you because I know where you have been!

Tears of Salt

Exotic jewellery wrapped around her arms
Belied the fullness of her charms
Her secret passage hidden still
She wandered through men's hearts at will

With eyes that burned to tell a tale
She danced the dance of the seventh veil
Conjuring spells from deep within
She satisfied her own lust for sin

On and on it went until
John the Baptist's head was still
Served on a plate then thrown on the floor
Herod's Dungeon breathed his breath no more

Shown to Jesus in the light
The Lord was summoned with all his might
King of the Jews admitted he
Before being tied to an orange tree

Persecuted lashed and garnished with thorns
His crown was sealed by a Devil with horns
Double-crossed he openly cried
Tears of salt for those who had lied

Tied untied and tied was he
Fated to die one two and three
The Chosen One was nailed to a cross
When the world suffered his agonising loss

Rome's mistake was to adorn a man
With immortality as only Rome can
Shocked betrayed and accused of treason
Isolated and searching for reason

Seven thousand miles away
In the desert of dreams a scribe passed away
After committing to gold the words he was given
By an angel sent as a man's heart was riven

The commandment to record on plates of gold
A gift to bestow when the elders grew old
Enough to guide a mortal man to proclaim
The imminent return of the one who was slain

John's promise to Jesus to announce to the world
That he would not die would be solemnly heard
A bell would ring and others would follow
Dispelling darkness with light at the dawn of a new tomorrow!

The Archangel

Who is for the birds
And who is for the Spring
Eternal youth is water
For whatever life may bring

I thunder through the graves of those who have gone astray
Dishonouring me and feloniously planting their seed the wrong way
As a consequence it will be twisted and malformed when it grows
Standing out in the crowds where imperfections show

To have sold your soul to the devil and invited him in
Is to have eaten bitter fruit and committed adultery within
The depths which you plundered will now swallow you whole
And your miserable life will be buried in a freshly dug hole

I do not seek revenge and a do not seek favour
But my sense of honour and duty does not waver
My moral fibre my ethics and my codes
Have stood the test of time when asked to carry the load

To the one place where you all must go
And be pinned to the crucifix for what you don't know
The eye of mercy will scrutinise your claim
To be set free and liberated in his holy name

If you decide that the honourable thing to do
Is to apologise for everything that you didn't do
Your salvation will be offered to you for a prayer in return
For the inconsequential loss suffered whilst you burn

I come to you as the archangel with a purpose in mind
That is to introduce you to others of my kind
You will see wisdom and love balanced with equal measure
To be given to you for all time to treasure

Accept the gifts freely with an open heart
And you will be free to make a new start
I will then give you my blessing to be on your way
To the reception you will receive after Judgment Day

A burnt offering and some fertile soil from the Valley of Kings
Was enough to bring pharaoh the water from eternal springs
My price for immortality is a small price to pay
If you value your seed don't let it wither away

Who is for the birds
And who is for the spring
Eternal youth is water
For whatever life may bring

Dreams

I'm constantly visited by angels it seems
Who fly through my thoughts and enter my dreams
Who could imagine a more peaceful pursuit
Than the one which I take as I follow the route

Through life's open door into the house of a man
Who builds a place to share memories as only he can
Up the staircase of remembrance I dance to the tune
Of heralds and cohorts from room to room

I gain strength from the music of life everyday
To enjoy the fruits of my efforts in this small way
Strange flights of fancy are permitted it seems
When buried deep within earthly dreams

Oh to be free to enact all these things
During the course of the next day and all that it brings
But for now I will slumber and give thanks for the time
That the spell lasts and I wait for the alarm bell to chime

When the angels depart and I wake every day
I will rise to the challenges come what may
To enrich and support the ones who need me
In their lives like the fruit from a new apple tree

Refreshed and renewed by an angels delight
In seeing me prosper and fight the good fight
A dream is for real when a promise comes true
So ask an angel for help and it will help you!

Iron in the Soul

As a voice cried out in the depths of night
The west wind blew with all its might
Carrying a message as a plea for trust
Lest all the world return to dust

Imprisoned in a dungeons keep
I search for ways to get to sleep
And bury all the dogs of war
Accumulated at my door

The world around the world I see
Is not the world I want to be
The one which nurtures not the just
But the kind of person who has needs must

As I grow old and bite from the tree
That grew so strong and kept me free
I'm conscious not to bite too hard
Lest it should fall a house of card

Better to defend a way
That shows you to your dying day
Ignoring truth is no excuse
To gain submission with abuse

If I took an inch and ran a mile
Would Satan's hook my soul defile
Fighting as I tried to free myself
Could I compete with someone else

I thunder through the graves of those
Whose seed has head and heart transposed
I don't need love and I don't need treason
To feel the need for one good reason

To expose the bloodlines that run green not red
Conceived to steal another's bread
By disregarding the rules laid down
On tablets of stone from holy ground

Oh to be the arbiter of dreams
And teach the truth of what being faithful means
If could do that I would sleep as one
With my own truths and be jealous of none

The Jolly Roger

Who am I to argue or to try to pass the blame
You knew what to expect when you played the game
It hasn't been a bed of roses I would say the same
But you went too far when you took my name in vain

You expected more I expected less
A balance is always better than a disproportionate mess
An animal knows better than to bite the hand that feeds
You called it just desserts I called it greed

To love cherish and nurture is what I heard you say
I said the same when I met you that day
It's easy to forget that as time goes marching on
If you give what you receive that's how to get along

If I gave you any more I would respect myself less
Bankrupting myself emotionally unless
I paid myself interest like a government loan
And kept it myself like a dog with his bone

Quid pro quo I would have loved to know why
You had to demean yourself by telling me a lie
Me I was born with an irresistible eye
Intent on not letting the world just sail by

It's not a bad thing to cut someone some slack
And say you go ahead I'm alright Jack
That way you can both be pirates in arms
Stealing kisses from others without doing harm

Affairs of the heart can be soon washed away
If its mutual consent that brought them your way
Don't deny magic if it's known to exist
But be careful to keep it shrouded in mist

Keep your Jolly Roger flying at half mast
In case you find yourself a victim of the past
Raise it only when the bountiful prize
Is irresistible to your roving eyes!

A Time to Live

Accept my trojan horse and never live a lie
Open up your heart to reason long before you die
Eat the truth of plenty do not stop to cry
Your happiness is in large measure if you will only try

I was your friend your companion and your rock
Long before you called my name and heard the crowing of the cock
When worlds collide and nothing seems to offer you a chance
Let me love you with a passion and offer you romance

I will love you every second every minute every hour
And the empty meadows will fill up with every kind of flower
The harvest fields will feed our bounty every single day
Enough to store up love and squirrel it away

The promises I make and the promises I keep
Stored up and remembered when we talk of what we reap
I am the embodiment of truth in everything I do
Ergo I wish to spend my life you

The Cheat

Drawing from strengths that I didn't know I had
And driven by the need to freeze out something bad
Cold blood ran through my naked body one day
As I metaphorically stripped my inhibitions away

To cleanse my soul from the stains of the shame
I prayed to wash away the ghost of her name
A ghost I had known to be devoid of all mercy
Lying to me consistently until I felt dirty

When a cold-blooded person looks you in the eye
It's enough to make you curl up shrivel and die
Their reptilian emotionless pursuit of a lie
Creates a bonfire of vanities and ultimately makes you cry

She started out like they all seem to do
Complaining about nothing but appearing to be blue
Asking for the Earth every working day
When nobody else was behaving in that way

Diamonds and pearls were never enough
Good clothes and fast cars and all that nice stuff
And of course a big house to store it all away
Like a squirrel on speed gathering up nuts in May

I wouldn't have minded except for the fact
That when I was away skiing she was caught in the act
Of cheating with someone who I thought was a friend
And creating a problem which was difficult to mend

The reason for straying was never discussed
Creating an atmosphere of ever present mistrust
Oh how I tried to bridge the abyss
That loomed in the background with every stolen kiss

I know now that she was torn away in a flash
By a meal at the Blue Monkey paid for with cash
You could say it was dirty money being spent to take aim
Calculated to usurp and steal from my domain

The guy who did this knowingly planned to appeal
To the feelings which women reluctantly feel
When they are seduced by a moment of clandestine pleasure
And cave in without thinking about that which they treasure

I have no idea if she now thinks of me at all
It's been 25 years with my back to the wall
Waiting for the next year to slowly pass away
Alone with those feelings with nothing more to say

The subject was apparently closed the day that she left
Having planned it to perfection leaving me bereft
How she can live with the guilt of doing that to me
Complicit with a monkey is disgusting to see

My thirst for alcohol dried up after she had gone
Cutting off the source of my solace like a gun
Aimed at my head to make me realise the gain
That I could make if my sobriety were to remain

I'm a much better person myself these days
Full of admiration and stoic praise
For those who can live with imperfections and marry
Someone whose bags they will now have to carry

I myself am content to live behind the glass
Avoiding the donkeys and worshipping the ass
Following the road like Muffin the mule
Funny but decidedly nobody's fool

I cast an eye to the future and reel in the past
But presently the anvil of time is my last
I walk in shoes made to compete at a pace of my choosing
A winner now with no real fear of losing

I am not the first and I will not be the last
To enjoy my own company with no longing for the past
My future is a healthy garden with no weeds to choke the seed
Of that which I will plant in the hourglass of my need

Only time will tell if a partner wants to play
The games that give us pleasure and oft dictate the way
A life unfolds then gently melts away
Forever keeping secrets until the Judgement Day!

Feeling Blue

If I could draw faces I would paint myself in blue
Not because I'm sad or looking for something to do
You see blue is my favourite colour and suits me people say
Art is quite a funny thing if it works in that particular way
If I only suit blue and that's the way I look
How can I express myself with colourful stories in a book
It's a mystery to me what colours really mean
So better left to artists who can mesmerise and dream
If all colours have meanings and they are put together well
The picture should be obvious to understand and tell
But all my pictures look like a motorway crash
And certainly wouldn't raise eyebrows or mountains of cash
So I will stick to my writing and just wearing something blue
And leave all the fancy stuff called art up to you
My art is a thing of great beauty to me
It's the wisdom behind everything that helps me to be
As colourful as a portrait fashioned by Picasso on the day
That he took a fancy to blue and painted me that way!

Lost Cause

What you did yesterday was a blessing in disguise
For the first time I realised that my love for you had died
I loved you for a reason which I wanted to share so much
My heart would have rejoiced to feel your tender touch
But the winds have changed and I feel the icy blast
Of a love now turned to snow a memory from the past
The love was pure innocent and real
How else could I have told you how I feel
The reality sunk in when I looked into your eyes
For a moment just a moment it made me realise
That life with you would have offered me the chance
To form a perfect union a heavenly romance
What I'm left with is a feeling that I should find another way
To bring a measure of happiness in to your every day

Only the Lonely

Reaching back through mists of convoluted time
I saw the ghost of loneliness sitting alongside mine
Holding within his withered hand a single blackened rose
A chapter left unfinished in a book about to close

The thorn of my squandered opportunities having pricked his conscience twice
The ghost was smiling to himself as he contemplated life
He was trying to console my unrequited grief
At having reached the end without turning over one more leaf

As blood dripped from the rose and life began to ebb away
His sunken eyes met mine and I thought I heard him say
"It's not for you to judge the time when mercy conquers pain
I bear that cross myself with a heart inscribed with your name"

I made a friend of loneliness that day my river died
Consequential loss washed away the bridge of sighs
Replacing it with a one-way street leading to an empty parking lot
No choice but to join the queue and try to stop the rot

A friendly smile seemed to overcome his face
Recognition of my state of altered grace
He blessed me with the stem that no one else could see
A naked flower to proclaim a pyric victory

With sadness spreading out like the shock wave from a crash
My inner being was touched by his act of selflessness
I wanted to embrace him and sooth his troubled mind
And cross the Rubicon to see what I could find

I searched my mind carefully to see if I could pray
And found the words which I am about to say
"Bless us both my friend and if eternity comes our way
We will ride the train of truth together beyond my dying day"

The thought that loneliness could vanish without a trace
Was anathema to me as I looked into his face
But like a sculptor carving granite I traced the outline of his hand
And took the rose from him just before he turned to sand

The flower seemed to breathe and change from black to pink
Its petals shone with moisture what was I to think?
I felt new life enter into my withered frame
Revitalised as if the ghost of loneliness had done the same

Kindred spirits now abandoning the pit
Aware that the Sword of Damocles was hanging over it
I left behind the noxious fumes of mortal loneliness
And became forever wedded to the flower of righteousness

If there is ever need to question right from wrong
Being moribund and not having the time to wait too long
I need only to remember the ghost that took away my pain
To be thankfully on the road to happiness again!

The Chameleon

As daybreak is to the chameleon I look towards the sun
My blood runs cold with ambitions left undone
You broke my heart today when you turned and slipped away
Your enigmatic face turning colours into grey
I see you differently as I watch you from afar
Your brilliance dimmed as if a fallen star
Your meaning lost to me on the bonfires that remain
When all the lights illuminate the sapphires of your name
Once approached a chameleon engorges to reveal
An appetite for life matched only by the way I feel
As I watch the cinders burn and cooling embers die
Forever known to me a chameleon says goodbye
Until awakened by the turning of the tides
The moon wipes away the sadness in my eyes
I am the chameleon of dedicated love
Through day and night a searchlight from above
The camouflage that cloaks my feelings and makes me disappear
Without a trace when enemies are near
Is one step forward and two steps back
A good solid defence that is better than attack!

The Fist of the Rose

Grab the stem with the hand
That feels less pain and understands
That love is just a rose's fist
Holding tight a perfumed mist
Yielding from the petal's skin
Thoughts from lovers coiled within
Abandoning their mortal chains
To unleash their dreams without refrain
Free to reach out and embrace
A promise made err it's too late
The moment frozen like a flower
On the breath of winter's coldest hour
What reason a rose without a smell
Or a fragrance born but not to tell
The progress of a life unfurled
Making sense of all the world
Imagine a field with seeds to grow
In the depth of darkness down below
Waiting patiently for the moment when
The light of fortune favours them
The seeds of life are in us all
We count the days until they fall
Like drops of rain to impregnate a field
With long memories that only graveyards yield
The humble seed gives rise to flower
The flower succumbs to the fist of power
Ground to dust in a cemetery parade
On the days when heroes salutes are made
The reason that the clenched fist of the rose
Holds power over us nobody knows
We cling on to that love until we die
And the rose is replaced with a solemn goodbye